JUN 0 5 2013

ONONDAGA COUNTY PUBLIC LIBRARY
THE GALLERIES OF SYRACUSE
447 S. SALINA STREET
SYRACUSE, NY 13202-2494
WWW.ONLIB.ORG

Barack Obama
44th U.S. President

CHANGE
WE NEED

written by Darlene R. Stille   illustrated by Richard Stergulz

Beginner
Biographies

Content Consultant:
Khalilah Brown-Dean, PhD, Peter Strauss Family Assistant
Professor of Political Science and African American Studies, Yale University

magic
wagon

visit us at www.abdopublishing.com

Published by Magic Wagon, a division of the ABDO Group, PO Box 398166, Minneapolis, MN 55439. Copyright © 2013 by Abdo Consulting Group, Inc. International copyrights reserved in all countries. All rights reserved. No part of this book may be reproduced in any form without written permission from the publisher.

Looking Glass Library™ is a trademark and logo of Magic Wagon.

Printed in the United States of America, North Mankato, Minnesota.
112012
012013

♻ THIS BOOK CONTAINS AT LEAST 10% RECYCLED MATERIALS.

Text by Darlene R. Stille
Illustrations by Richard Stergulz
Edited by Holly Saari
Series design by Emily Love
Cover and interior production by Craig Hinton

Library of Congress Cataloging-in-Publication Data

Stille, Darlene R.
  Barack Obama : 44th U.S. President / written by Darlene R. Stille ; illustrated by Richard Stergulz ; content consultant: Khalilah Brown-Dean.
     p. cm. – (Beginner biographies)
  "Looking Glass Library."
  Includes index.
  ISBN 978-1-61641-939-4
  1. Obama, Barack–Juvenile literature. 2. Presidents–United States–Biography–Juvenile literature. 3. African Americans–Biography–Juvenile literature. I. Stergulz, Richard, ill. II. Title.
  E908.S85 2013
  973.932092–dc23
   [B]
                                                                  2012023800

Table of Contents

The Birth of a Future President

On August 4, 1961, a future president of the United States was born in Honolulu, Hawaii. His parents named him Barack Hussein Obama Jr. The name *Barack* comes from Swahili, an African language. The word means "blessing."

Barack's parents were excited to have a baby boy.

Barack's Childhood

Barack's father, Barack Hussein Obama Sr., was born in Kenya. Barack's mother, Ann Dunham, was born in Kansas. The two had met at college in Hawaii.

When Barack was still a baby, his father left. He went to study at a different college. Barack's father later returned to Kenya. Barack's parents divorced when Barack was two. He did not see his father much while growing up.

In the 1960s, many people thought it was wrong for a black person and a white person to marry. But Ann and Barack Sr. did not think so. They believed that black people and white people were equal.

Barack spent a lot of time with his mother when he was growing up.

It was important to Ann that Barack had a good education.

Barack lived with his mother and grandparents in Honolulu. He loved them very much. He called his grandmother "Toot" and his grandfather "Gramps."

When Barack was six years old, Ann married another college student. He was from Indonesia, a country in Southeast Asia. Barack moved with his mother and new stepfather to Indonesia. Soon he had a sister named Maya.

Ann adored her son. She wanted him to do well in school. She woke him up at 4:30 in the morning to teach him reading and writing. Sometimes he complained. One time she told him, "This is no picnic for me either, Buster." Then he stopped complaining.

In Hawaii, Barack spent a lot of time with Toot and Gramps. One of their favorite things to do together was to go to the beach.

Barack and his father got to know each other better during his father's visit.

A Visit from His Father

Ann decided that Barack should go to school in the United States. When he was ten, he went to live with Gramps and Toot in Hawaii.

Barack knew about his father only from stories his mother had told him. He knew that his father had grown up in a poor country. His father had won scholarships to study in the United States. After school, Barack Sr. went back to Kenya to help the people there. Shortly after Barack moved back to Hawaii, his father came to visit him.

During the visit, Barack learned that his father had a new family in Kenya. Barack heard about his six Kenyan brothers and one sister. Then his father returned to Africa. The visit was the last time Barack saw his father.

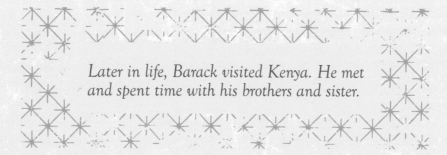

Later in life, Barack visited Kenya. He met and spent time with his brothers and sister.

Finding His Place

Barack attended Punahou School in Honolulu. He was a good student. He played on the school's basketball team. His teammates called him "Barry O'Bomber" because he was good at making jump shots far from the basket.

People of many races lived in Hawaii. Barack had many classmates who were not white. But still, he wasn't sure how he fit in with his peers. He was part white and part black. He tried hard to understand who he was.

Barack loved playing basketball.

13

After high school, Obama went to college in Los Angeles, California, and in New York City, New York. He became interested in public affairs. He wanted to learn how the government could better help its citizens. So he decided to study political science.

The unfairness in the world troubled Obama. He wanted leaders to take action. He participated in demonstrations. One was against racism in South Africa.

Onondaga County Public Library
Syracuse, New York

Obama and others wanted black people in South Africa to be treated equally.

FREEDOM

EQUAL RIGHTS IN SOUTH AFRICA

EQUAL RIGHTS

STO ACI

AFRICA

Community Organizer

Obama graduated from Columbia University in 1983. He wanted to help make people's lives better. For the next three years, he worked as a community organizer in the South Side of Chicago, Illinois. This area was home to many poor African Americans.

Obama wanted to make changes that would last. He wanted to fix the problems that were keeping the neighborhood poor. He worked to improve schools and help people get better jobs.

Obama gathered people's signatures so he could make changes in the community.

Obama studied hard to do well in law school.

Law School

Obama wanted to learn another way to change the unfairness he saw around him. He decided to become a lawyer. In law school, he would learn more ways to help others.

In 1988, Obama moved to Massachusetts to attend Harvard Law School. In his third year, he was elected president of the *Harvard Law Review*. This was a very big honor. The journal had been in print for more than 100 years. Obama became the first African American ever to be its president.

Starting a Family

    While in law school, Obama took a summer job at a Chicago law firm. Michelle Robinson was also working there. The two began to date and fell in love. Once Obama graduated from Harvard, he moved to Chicago to be with Michelle. Soon after, they got married.

Barack and Michelle married in 1992.

21

The Obamas enjoy spending time together.

Barack and Michelle decided it was time to start a family. In 1998, the couple's first daughter was born. They named her Malia.

In 2001, they had another daughter. They named her Natasha, or Sasha, for short. Barack and Michelle both had full-time jobs. But they also found time to spend with their daughters.

Millions of people heard Obama's speech at the 2004 Democratic National Convention.

A Political Leader

Obama worked as a lawyer for four years. He helped make sure voting was fair for everyone. He also taught at the University of Chicago Law School.

In 1996, Obama ran for the Illinois Senate and won. In 2004, Obama was elected to be a U.S. senator. In these jobs, Obama worked to pass laws that improved education and helped poor people.

Many political leaders started to notice him. They invited Obama to give an important speech at the 2004 Democratic National Convention. His speech was a huge success. After this, he became well known by many people.

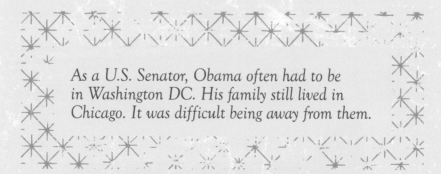

As a U.S. Senator, Obama often had to be in Washington DC. His family still lived in Chicago. It was difficult being away from them.

Many Americans believed Obama would be a good president.

Obama saw many things in the United States that he thought could be better. Many Americans could not afford to visit the doctor. He thought all Americans should have health care. Many scientists believed burning oil was harming the planet. He thought there could be cleaner fuel than oil.

In 2007, Obama decided to run for president so he could help make these changes. He traveled around the country making speeches. He asked Americans everywhere to vote for him. In November 2008, they chose him to be the next president.

President Obama

On January 20, 2009, Obama became the forty-fourth president of the United States. He was the first African American ever to hold the office.

Obama worked hard to be a good president. He helped people get jobs and have health care. He also worked to improve America's relationship with other countries.

In 2012, Obama ran for a second term. The people of the United States felt he was doing a good job. He was reelected on November 6, 2012. He will continue to work hard for all Americans.

As president, Obama is very busy.
But he still makes time for his family.

FUN FACTS

✦ Obama has written two books about his life, *Dreams from My Father* and *The Audacity of Hope*.

✦ In October 2009, Obama received a great honor. He was awarded the Nobel Peace Prize because he worked to improve peace and cooperation among nations.

✦ During his run for president, Obama promised his daughters a dog. In April 2009, a black Portuguese water dog named Bo joined the family at the White House.

TIMELINE

1961 Barack Hussein Obama Jr. was born on August 4 in Honolulu, Hawaii.

1967 Obama moved to Indonesia with his mother and stepfather.

1971 Obama moved back to Hawaii to live with his grandparents and attend school.

1983 Obama graduated from Columbia University with a bachelor's degree in political science.

1983 Obama became a community organizer in Chicago.

1992 Obama married Michelle Robinson.

1996 Obama was elected an Illinois state senator.

2004 Obama was elected to the U.S. Senate.

2009 Obama became the first African-American president of the United States.

GLOSSARY

community organizer—a person who works to help people, often in poor neighborhoods.

Democratic National Convention—a national meeting held every four years. During the convention, the Democratic Party chooses its candidates for president and vice president.

demonstration—a group of people joining together to protest something.

health care—medical services and people that work to keep people healthy.

law firm—a company that hires lawyers to handle law cases.

lawyer—a person who studies law and then works with laws.

political leader—a person elected to serve in government.

political science—the study of public affairs.

race—a group of people having the same skin color or other physical traits.

racism—the belief that one race is better than another.

scholarship—money to help pay for a student's schooling.

senator—a person elected to serve in the senate of a state or of the United States.

LEARN MORE

At the Library

Cook, Michelle. *Our Children Can Soar: A Celebration of Rosa, Barack, and the Pioneers of Change*. New York: Bloomsbury, 2009.

Grimes, Nikki. *Barack Obama: Son of Promise, Child of Hope*. New York: Simon & Schuster Books for Young Readers, 2008.

Winter, Jonah. *Barack*. New York: Katherine Tegen, 2008.

On the Web

To learn more about Barack Obama, visit ABDO Group online at **www.abdopublishing.com**. Web sites about Obama are featured on our Book Links page. These links are routinely monitored and updated to provide the most current information available.

INDEX